DIESELS ON EASTERN REGION

DIESELS ON EASTERN REGION

NORMAN E. PREEDY

D. BRADFORD BARTON LIMITED

Frontispiece Close to the slow-flowing River Deben between Wickham Market and Melton in East Suffolk, English Electric No. 37 034 heads for Liverpool Street with the 09.46 from Lowestoft on an August morning in 1974. [G. R. Mortimer]

ISBN 0 85153 202 0

printed in Great Britain by Chapel River Press (IPC Printers), Andover
for the publishers

D. BRADFORD BARTON LTD · Trethellan House · Truro · Cornwall · England

introduction

Along with the West Country, East Anglia was selected by British Railways as one of the pilot areas for the introduction of diesels, in the mid 1950's. As is now well-known, Western Region opted for diesel-hydraulics, whilst Eastern Region initially received two principal classes of diesel-electrics. These were the Type 4 English Electric 2000hp units later known as Class 40, and the smaller Type 2 Brush 1365hp (Mirrlees-engined) units, subsequently Class 31. In contrast to the West Country, the reception of these new diesels was very favourable on the ex-GE main line, and the Class 40s were soon making child's play of the existing loads and timings of such expresses as 'The East Anglian' and 'The Norfolkman'. With eleven bogies on, they accomplished the two-hour run to Norwich with power to spare, including the Ipswich stop. Despite the fact that this GE main line is not the billiard-table route that might be imagined—Brentwood bank for example has three miles or so on an adverse 1 in 100, and 1 in 84 at the steepest point—even the Class 31 locomotives were able to rival the work being done by 'Britannia' Pacifics on comparable services.

The programme on the GE section was to replace an existing fleet of 668 steam locomotives with 249 main line diesels and by the summer of 1959, just over one hundred main line units were in use from ER sheds (44 Hornsey, 38 Stratford, 14 March, 4 Norwich, 2 Ipswich) —twelve months later more than 200 were in service, with less than half the passenger or freight services operated by the old form of motive power. Dieselisation spread rapidly too on to the GN section, gradually moving northwards. By the end of 1960 Class 40s and the Pacifics were sharing the working of the main expresses and putting up very comparable performances. What was noticeable to the operating authorities was the uplift in morale in each area with the introduction of diesels. Teething troubles and unreliability at this date were, however, major factors in the transitional period between steam and diesel, as may be judged by the fact that works fitters were sent out not only on the locomotives selected for Royal Train duty but as a precaution also on any other trains preceding it. The prevalence of minor breakdowns, however, could not mask the great overall economy that diesel traction had brought and the fact that by 1960, the best Class 40s were putting up annual mileages of 140,000, which was twice that of an 'A3'.

The introduction of the 1650hp Class 37s from English Electric filled the gap between the 40s and 31s for freight and intermediate Type 3 duties, whilst the Class 47, with 2750hp on tap, when they became available in the early 1960s made possible a considerable acceleration in services. DMUs had inevitably spread across the numerous lightly-trafficked branches surviving from NE and pre-grouping days, although the Beeching 'axe' saw the end of many of these, particularly in sparsely-populated East Anglia. The coming of the extremely successful Class 55 twin-engined 'Deltics' from English Electric, with their 3300hp and 100mph capability, gave the greatest boost to East Coast main line services after their introduction in 1961; they give results comparable to that achieved by electrification on the West Coast main line at unbelievably greater cost.

As regards the future, once the 'Deltics' are phased-out, super-power Class 47 diesels will probably become the ER flagships, backed up by the very efficient and wide-ranging normal Class 47s on all but the fastest Inter-City services. The Class 31s have been re-engined in line with the Class 37s and these two types, plus some Class 25s, will continue to handle other subsidiary passenger and freight services in the foreseeable future. With increasing standardisation the number of different classes has declined—and the amount of inter-Regional use of locomotives increased—to the extent that it now seems hard to believe how many different classes once worked on Eastern Region. The BTH 82xx class; the 59xx 'Baby Deltics'; the early Class 24s in East Anglia; the 533xx class which later went to Scottish Region; all are now only a memory as standardisation proceeds.

5A28
D5678

Introduced in 1957, to spearhead dieselisation on Eastern Region, the Brush Class 31 diesel-electrics were 1250hp units (later re-engined) with A1A-A1A wheel arrangement. D5607, seen on 26 April 1961, typifies the change-over from steam then well under way; 'A3' Class Pacific No. 60111 *Enterprise* is in attendance, under the coal chute at Kings Cross. [G. A. Richardson]

Class 31 D5678 on empty stock working at Kings Cross—a night scene on 6 February 1971. Movement of a lamp near the leading end of the first coach during uncoupling shows the lengthy period of exposure required for photographs under dimly lit conditions such as these, in this case 30 seconds at F8. [Norman E. Preedy]

D 5651
WAITING ROO
PLATFORMS

Brush Class 47 units, with the bigger 'Deltics', form the backbone of motive power for ER long distance passenger services: No. 1992, from Gateshead depot, at rest alongside the old No. 5 Platform at Kings Cross with the 10.30 from Newcastle. [Norman E. Preedy]

Another of the Class 31s, D5651, under the graceful roof at Kings Cross, waiting to back out with empty Pullman stock for the carriage sidings. These locomotives looked extremely smart in their original striped green livery, with grey roof, a paintwork scheme that suited their lines far better than the present day blue and yellow. [G. A. Richardson]

The powerful Class 55 'Deltics' are the flagship class of diesel on Eastern Region, a batch of twenty-two 3300hp Co-Co units put into service in 1961, built by English Electric. They have become justifiably famous for their power and speed, and for putting up extremely high annual mileages as a result of intense rostering. In fact they replaced more than three times the number of Pacifics doing similar duties in steam days. Above: No. 9006 *The Fife and Forfar Yeomanry* rests by the buffer stops on a winter night in 1962 after a fast run from Newcastle. [Norman E. Preedy]. Opposite: No. 9001 *St. Paddy* about to leave the terminus with the 22.15 'Night Aberdonian', 5 November 1973.

[Brian Morrison]

1S70

One of the hallmarks of a 'Deltic' hard at work is the noticeable exhaust created by the pair of two-stroke Napier engines which provide their power; here No. 55 021 *Argyll and Sutherland Highlander* is exerting near-maximum tractive effort up the 1 in 107 at the exit to Copenhagen Tunnel with the down 'Aberdonian' in June 1974.
[P. A. Dobson]

Another scene on the north side of Copenhagen Tunnel just outside Kings Cross, with a Class 31 with an electrification works train approaching the flyover crossing the main lines. This higher line and its tunnel portal is also seen on the opposite page. [P. A. Dobson]

Class 31/2 No. 5568 heads down the bank into Copenhagen Tunnel with a semi-fast from Cambridge, 22 March 1973. Her original 1250hp Mirrlees engiñe was replaced by a 1470 EE unit in 1967, the re-engining of the class taking place from 1966–68. [Brian Morrison]

The 'Deltics' are unmistakeable, to look at and to hear—No. 9020 *Nimbus* accelerating hard up the gradient towards Holloway with the 'Leeds Executive', shortly after its departure from Kings Cross at 15.55, 12 September 1973. [Brian Morrison]

1L22

1969
1B66

Class 31/2 No. 5612 passing Holloway South down signal box with a train of road stone from Kings Cross goods yard. [Brian Morrison]

Still in two-tone green livery, Class 47 No. 1969 with an up express amid typical inner London brickwork at Belle Isle, between Copenhagen and Gasworks tunnels, 22 March 1973. [Brian Morrison]

A close-up of 'Deltic' No. 55 013 *The Black Watch* running light under the Caledonian Road overbridge at Holloway on a June morning in 1974. She is one of the class allocated to Edinburgh (Haymarket) depot. [P. A. Dobson]

Old-style Pullman cars have now disappeared from the ER scene, and Class 40 locomotives are no longer common on the ex-GN main line. In October 1958, D206 has charge of the eight-car set making up the southbound 'Master Cutler', passing Holloway on the last mile or so of the run from Sheffield. [Brian Morrison]

1A16

Another of the numerous ER-allocated Class 47s storms round the curve at New Southgate with a down Newcastle express on a June afternoon in 1974. [P. A. Dobson]

In contrast to the former scene, a photograph taken fifteen years later (in March 1973) of the contemporary 'Yorkshire Pullman' bound for Kings Cross behind Class 47 No. 1519. [Brian Morrison]

Scenes at Wood Green, 23rd June 1973; Class 31/1 No. 5623 on the down through line with a seven-coach train and (below) Class 47 No. 1111 makes light work of a Skegness–Kings Cross express.
[Norman E. Preedy]

A 'Deltic' picks up speed again after a p.w. slack near New Southgate, heading a late-running express from Bradford and Leeds towards Kings Cross. The figure apparently balanced on the locomotive roof is in fact working on the overhead wiring above.
[P. A. Dobson]

1B66

1A50

Heading an interesting selection of coaches, 'Baby Deltic' D5906 is on a Cambridge–Kings Cross semi-fast at Ganwick, 17 August 1961. She was one of the ten units in Class 23, built by English Electric, and was withdrawn in 1968. [Derek Cross]

Hadley Wood station, September 1960: Class 20 D8045 on a lowly but nevertheless useful task—heading refuse disposal wagons back empty to London and (below) Class 40 D203 on the down 'Talisman' bound for Edinburgh. Both these locomotives are now allocated to Midland Region. [Derek Cross]

The experimental 2800hp diesel-electric D0280 *Falcon*, built by Brush and fitted with two Maybach high-speed engines, originally worked on Eastern Region before transfer to the West of England. She is seen here near Potters Bar in 1962 on the 'Tyne-Tees Pullman'.
[Norman E. Preedy]

The familiar front-end of a Class 47 catches the sunlight at the south portal of the Welwyn Tunnels, hurrying an up express towards Kings Cross in April 1974.
[P. A. Dobson]

A return to Liverpool Street and the Great Eastern line, where dieselisation on ER first began; Class 47 No. 1778 starting the 10.30 for Norwich, 3 September 1970. [G. R. Mortimer]

The uncompromisingly ugly but functional front end of a Class 37, seen at Liverpool Street. The contrast in appearance between this English Electric design and that of their diesel-hydraulic equivalents, the Hymeks, is a marked one. No. 37 034 is one of the variants in this numerous class with the greatest amount of 'clutter'—notably split headcode panels, extra ventilators, and gangway doors. [P. A. Dobson]

A trio of BR Class 08 six-coupled shunters in well-kept condition shuttle through Stratford en route to shunting duties, June 1974. Nowhere has the move towards complete standardisation been more evident than amongst the BR fleet of shunting locomotives, which once comprised over 2000 units of well over twenty different classes and sub-classes. [P. A. Dobson]

English Electric-built No. 40 158 running light through Stratford yard. [P. A. Dobson]

The Class 37s have given good service on Eastern Region, both on passenger and freight services, but principally the latter. The great majority of the 300 or more in the class are at work on ER duties, allocated to Gateshead, Tinsley, Stratford and elsewhere. Here, No. 37 032, newly repainted and with a well turned-out rake of six coaches, passes through Stratford with a Norwich–Liverpool Street express, in May 1974. [P. A. Dobson]

An earlier scene on the ex-GE main line in east London, with Class 40 D202 on a down Norwich express, 6 August 1958. The first of these big 2000hp diesel-electrics came to Stratford that year and rapidly established a good reputation for themselves. They are now regarded as more of an LM Region type but 50 or so are still allocated to ER, principally at Gateshead, York, and Healey Mills (Wakefield). [Brian Morrison]

The introduction of the Type 3 1750hp Class 37s enabled the Class 40s to be moved to more demanding duties elsewhere. No. 6968, from Stratford depot, shows her abilities on Brentwood bank with the down 'Scandinavian' for Harwich, Parkeston Quay. [Brian Morrison]

Another scene on the 1 in 103 of Brentwood bank, with Class 31/2 No. 5634 heading a parcels train for Parkeston Quay, 26 April 1973. [Brian Morrison]

WHISTLE
1F28
6968

6F22

1N17

One of the Ford Motor Company's Freightliners, from Halewood to Parkeston Quay, heads down the GE main line across the viaduct over the River Ter near Hatfield Peverel, 28 May 1971.
[G. R. Mortimer]

One of the ER fleet of Class 47s, No. 1756, races down Brentwood bank with an express from Norwich in April 1972. With 2750hp available, these units have more than ample power for services to and from East Anglia.
[Brian Morrison]

A Metro-Cammel two-coach d.m.u. on the Witham–Maldon branch, near Wickham Bishops station, 23 August 1964. The end of passenger services over this branch came early the following month and the track has now been lifted. Note the timber trestle construction of this low viaduct. [G. R. Mortimer]

A scene on the Stour Valley branch near Colchester, with the 07.52 Sudbury–Marks Tey about to depart from the distinctive station of Chappel & Wakes Colne, on 14 June 1969. This station is now the home of the Stour Valley Railway Preservation Society. [G. R. Mortimer]

Class 40 D204 on the up 'East Anglian' passing soon-to-be-redundant steam power outside Colchester shed on a June day in 1958. At this point the electrified line to Clacton diverges to the right. [J. R. Besley]

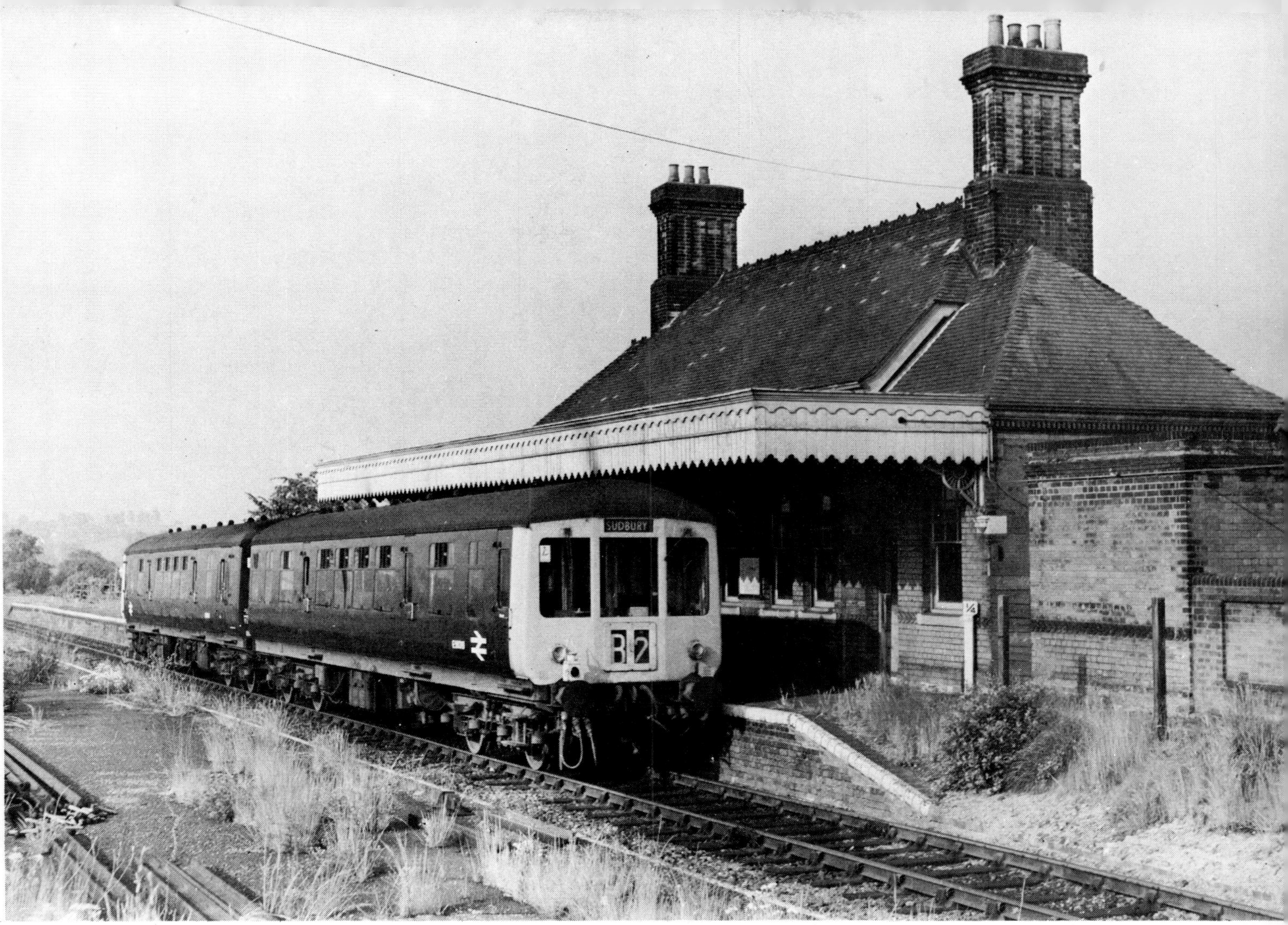
SUDBURY
B2

Class 37 No. 6967 crossing Manningtree South Viaduct at the head of a Norwich–Liverpool Street train in May 1971. This tidal section of the River Stour here marks the boundary of Essex and Suffolk. [G. R. Mortimer]

Upper quadrants still add interest to the scene at Ipswich where a Class 37 accelerates away from the station on the curve past the marshalling yard with an express for the North of England, July 1974. [Malcolm Dunnett]

Class 31 D5699 at Bentley Junction, south of Ipswich, with the daily freight from the latter yard for the Hadleigh branch—a photograph taken in April 1965 in the last few days of services. D5699 was a regular on Royal Trains to and from Sandringham. [G. R. Mortimer]

Class 47 D1528 leaving Ipswich with the 15.40 to Liverpool Street on 10 August 1968. [G. R. Mortimer]

Class 40s at Ipswich, in the Brunswick Green era for diesels: newly introduced D205 alongside the platform on 2 August 1958 (above) and D202 entering the station with the down 'East Anglian' on 23 May of the same year. [J. R. Besley]

D205

40
D202

A view of Ipswich freight yard, July 1974; apart from an 08 Class shunter on the left, all six of the other diesels to be seen are of Class 31. These form the staple motive power for most freight working in East Anglia and with its gradual decline, the over-abundance of these Brush units has been responsible for their move to other parts of the country, notably to Western Region. [Malcolm Dunnett]

A Class 47 runs into Ipswich with a south-bound train, July 1972. The Class 31 in the foreground still wears the original striped green livery. [Malcolm Dunnett]

EE Class 37 D6714 on a Saturday in June 1965 near Wickham Market with a Yarmouth–Liverpool Street extra. The ex-GE line through East Suffolk was then much busier than now, with holiday traffic each summer. [G. R. Mortimer]

At Saxmundham Junction, the branch to Aldeburgh diverges from the GE main line. Class 31 D5531 is on the up main with empty stock, September 1966. Closed now to passenger traffic, the Aldeburgh branch is still open for freight as far as Sizewell. [G. R. Mortimer]

The BR Derby–Sulzer Type 2s, later known as the Class 24s, were amongst the first of the diesels to reach East Anglia but later were moved elsewhere. D5037, in pristine condition ex works and smart in the dark green/light green/grey livery that well suited all BR diesels, is about to leave Halesworth with a Saturdays-only Yarmouth–Liverpool Street train, September 1965. [G. R. Mortimer]

After some desultory shunting at Fakenham in Norfolk with the daily freight, Class 31 No. 5633 makes a start back for Norwich, 6 September 1971. Once passenger services continued beyond here to Wells-on-Sea but no longer, as with so many other of the considerable network of single line branches that criss-crossed the county. [G. R. Mortimer]

The deserted station at Audley End, approximately mid-way between Bishops Stortford and Cambridge, with a Class 37 passing through in charge of a train of oil tanks. [P. A. Dobson]

At Swavesey on the Cambridge to St. Ives branch, the driver of the d.m.u. hands back the single-line token to the signalman. A few weeks later, in the autumn of 1970, passenger services ceased over this line which was kept open for freight use. The unit is a two-coach Gloucester RCW, with motor-brake second E50339 leading. [G. R. Mortimer]

A contrast to the preceding d.m.u. scene on a quiet branch—'Deltic' No. 55 008 *The Green Howards* heading north at a steady ninety through St. Neots, with the ten-coach 'Yorkshire Pullman' (17.05 Kings Cross to Leeds) on 31 July 1974. [Philip D. Hawkins]

A haze of hot exhaust from Class 47/4 No. 47 516 about to rattle the platform fittings at Huntingdon as she storms through with the 11.47 Kings Cross to Newcastle, July 1974.
[Philip D. Hawkins]

March, at the meeting point of lines from Spalding, Peterborough, Wisbech and Cambridge, was formerly a busy junction, as the length and number of its platforms testify. Alas, the number of passengers handled has greatly declined, although freight traffic passing through has been less affected. Here Class 31 D5579 has just brought in a Harwich to Peterborough train on 15 July 1970. [Norman E. Preedy]

Class 31/2 No. 5820, from Sheffield Tinsley, with a ballast train near March, July 1970. In the background can be seen March m.p.d. and Whitemoor marshalling yard. [Norman E. Preedy]

1G70
5B00

8B33

Class 46 D185 passing Peterborough North signal box with a southbound train of cement hoppers, 14 June 1969.
[Norman E. Preedy]

Class 31 No. 5669, approaching Peterborough with a southbound Freightliner special, passes the exit from New England yards where No. 5611 waits to follow the 'Five B Zero Zero', the 13.10 to Holloway Carriage Sidings. In the background another Class 31, sporting headcode 8Z10, has just uncoupled from a fourth of these very useful Type 2 locomotives; 25 August 1973. [Norman E. Preedy]

A Class 25 passing through the new Peterborough station platforms with a train of empties from Whitemoor Yard for the Midland Region. Peterborough was the one-time 'bottleneck' on the East Coast where expresses had to observe a severe speed restriction because of curves. With the opening of the new station, the speed limit has been raised to 100mph. [Norman E. Preedy]

Class 47 No. 1108 heads the 16.15 from Kings Cross to York into the old down platform at Peterborough. Before complete remodelling of the layout, all expresses, whether calling at Peterborough or not, had to reduce speed severely over the sharp curves at each end of the station. [Norman E. Preedy]

1L29

278
UNAUTHORISED PERSONS MUST NOT USE THIS CROSSING

1577
1A2
W

Class 47 No. 47 046 with the 15.15 Manchester Piccadilly to Parkeston Quay at speed near Little Bytham, south of Grantham, on 17 August 1974. The embankment visible behind formerly carried the now disused ex-M & GN line from Spalding to Melton Mowbray. [G. A. Richardson]

Scenes at Grantham: above, Class 40 No. 278, from York depot, with a Leeds–Kings Cross train on 4 October 1972; below, Class 47 No. 1577, on 7 September 1973, with insect-spattered front end after long fast runs during the hot summer weeks of August of that year. [Norman E. Preedy]

Well-kept Class 55 No. 9001 *St. Paddy* at speed up Stoke bank through Little Bytham, making light work of the 1 in 200 up to Stoke Box with the down 'Talisman', 15 August 1973. No. 9001, with what seems at first a lugubrious name, is one of the Finsbury Park-allocated 'Deltics', which are named after famous racehorses. [Philip D. Hawkins]

Although the 'Deltics' have a good—indeed enviable—record for reliability in service, they fail on occasion. Here the 07.45 Kings Cross to Newcastle, running an hour or more late, approaches Grantham behind Class 31 No. 31 225 and ailing 'Deltic' No. 55 009 *Alycidon*, on an October day in 1974. The former had been commandeered from a ballast train at Peterborough. [Philip D. Hawkins]

The 13.35 Leeds to Kings Cross emerges from a fog-shrouded landscape near Retford on 3 April 1974 behind 'Deltic' No. 55 009 *Alycidon*. Weather conditions such as this illustrate the need for high-visibility colour-light signals if schedules are to be maintained. *Alycidon* is seen here experimentally fitted with twin headlights in place of the normal train indicators. [Philip D. Hawkins]

A pair of Class 31s, Nos. 5594 and 5685, ease through Grantham with a long ballast train, 22 August 1972. Since being re-engined with 1470hp EE 12-cylinder engines, these Brush-built Type 2s have been extremely reliable. [Norman E. Preedy]

Class 40 No. 40 177 at Sleaford with the 08.48 (S.O.) Manchester Piccadilly–Skegness, 10 August 1974.
[Revd. G. B. Wise]

Class 31s at Lincoln Central, 14 July 1973: No. 5811 is departing with a Manchester Piccadilly to Yarmouth relief, whilst No. 5518 waits to take over and work forward another train on the same service.
[Revd. G. B. Wise]

Derby-built twin unit No. E50024 and E56034, forming the 14.55 from Sheffield, passing High Street box on the approach to Lincoln Central on 21 March 1973.
[Revd. G. B. Wise]

A Class 25 from Tinsley depot, No. 5229, arriving at Lincoln Central with a train from Manchester. [Revd. G. B. Wise]

Class 31/2s Nos. 5547 and 5630 passing Branston in Lincolnshire on the GN/GE joint line with a freight for Whitemoor, March 1973. [Revd. G. B. Wise]

A harsh wintry sun glints along the flanks of Class 46 No. 46 029, re-starting from Doncaster with a Kings Cross–Leeds express on 25 November 1973. Near here, at Shaftholme Junction, was the division point between the old North Eastern and Eastern Regions before these were amalgamated in 1967. [Brian Morrison]

Class 47 No. 1882 on the through road at Doncaster with a block train of bogie oil tanks, 18 October 1972. Ten of these 100-tonners represent a load that would have been regarded as exceptional in steam days.
[Norman E. Preedy]

The up 'Flying Scotsman' approaching Doncaster in November 1973 behind 'Deltic' No. 9007 *Pinza*. Below, Class 31 No. 31 323 at the same location with a loose-coupled freight from Healey Mills to Hexthorpe. [Brian Morrison]

1E05

9D78

D6112

D5901

One of the named Class 40s, No. 40 027 *Parthia* at Guide Bridge on the ex-GC/LNW line with a train of cement hoppers, 19 March 1974. [Norman E. Preedy]

Until they were banished to Scotland, some of the unsuccessful NBL Class 29 Type 2s were put to work on Eastern Region; D6112 and D6110 are seen at Doncaster works in May 1959. Equally unsuccessful—for no very good reason, for they were a small single-engined edition of the much bigger 'Deltics'—were the units in Class 23; D5901 was also at Doncaster works on delivery at the same date. [Brian Morrison]

5820

A pair of Class 31s at Sheffield (Midland) on a return excursion from Mablethorpe show the two types of livery the class have known in their years of service. At the date of this photograph in June 1970, more or less equal numbers of the class could be seen in the original green and the later blue liveries.
[Norman E. Preedy]

A study in shadow and sunlight at Huddersfield, with a Class 45 about to start away with the 07.50 Newcastle–Liverpool in March 1971. These big Derby Sulzer 'Peaks' of Class 45 or 46 on Eastern Region are allocated to Leeds (Holbeck) and Gateshead; the cross-country services to Lancashire and to the West Country are their usual province. [Malcolm Dunnett]

Her two Napier engines somewhat out of tune, 'Deltic' D9011 *The Royal Northumberland Fusiliers* raises a cloud of exhaust fumes as she gets under way from Leeds (Central) in June 1961 with a train for Kings Cross. She is in the early two-tone green livery which most observers agree was more suited to their appearance than the present combination of blue and yellow. [J. R. Carter]

Since they entered service the 'Deltics' have always been seen on the East Coast main line and only rarely off the Kings Cross–Edinburgh (or Aberdeen) and Leeds routes. Two of the class traverse Midland Region metals at Salford, returning to North Eastern Region in the summer of 1961 after attention at Vulcan Foundry, Newton-le-Willows. [J. R. Carter]

Two winter scenes amid the Yorkshire countryside at Monk Fryston, north of Pontefract in November 1973: above, Class 47 No. 47 302 showing her capabilities with a fast-moving block train of 25 chemical hoppers, and (below) No. 46 045 heading for Newcastle with a down express. [Brian Morrison]

6E81

1E32

Still with gleaming paintwork after only a few miles running following out-shopping from Doncaster, English Electric Class 37 No. 37 238 passes through Selby station on the through road with a Doncaster–York parcels train, 14 June 1974. [Brian Morrison]

A Swindon-built d.m.u. with E51954, a motor-composite of Class 124/1 leading, pauses at Selby with one of the Trans-Pennine services to Manchester. A pair of Class 37s, Nos. 37 085 leading No. 37 216, add to the interest of the scene as they rumble through with a heavy drag of coal hoppers. [Brian Morrison]

1
1E59
8G
14

EE Class 20 No. 8024 entering York with a freight off the Scarborough line, 13 July 1971. Although familiar enough on Midland Region, only a few of these Type 1 units are based on ER depots, principally Sheffield (Tinsley). [Norman E. Preedy]

Scenes at York in July 1972: above, train 1V98, 16.30 Newcastle to Bristol, waiting to leave behind WR Class 46 No. 142 working back to her home shed at Bath Road; below, adding a much more authentic Eastern Region touch, Class 31/2 No. 5587 passing through with a loose-coupled freight. [Norman E. Preedy]

IV 98

8K10

1S35

Old and new outside York in August 1960; Class 40 D248 getting into her stride with a southbound express and Class J72 0-6-0T No. 68677 shunting empty coaching stock. [P. J. Lynch]

Class 40s are now only a memory on top-link East Coast services, their 2000hp being well below what is required for the speed of present day services, and the need for rapid recovery after out-of-course checks. Even Class 47s find it hard to cope with the standards set in this respect by the more powerful Class 55s; No. 9006 *The Fife and Forfar Yeomanry* at York on 18 July 1972 with a Kings Cross–Aberdeen train.
[Norman E. Preedy]

The massive girder bridge that spans all the six or more running tracks just south of York station forms a backdrop for Class 46 No. 148 notching up with a Newcastle–Kings Cross express on 18 July 1972.
[Norman E. Preedy]

1 A 24

The Derby-Sulzer Class 25s are much less ubiquitous on Eastern Region than on LM Region but Gateshead depot have a number on allocation; No. 25 046 potters along the down slow line near Thirsk with a nicely mixed freight on 13 June 1974. [Brian Morrison]

General freight traffic on the northern section of Eastern Region is still heavy, despite the overall decline in the production of coal, and tanker traffic is of increasing importance; Class 37 No. 37 167 heads north past Thirsk with one of the frequently seen block trains of tank wagons for Teesside, 13 June 1974. [Brian Morrison]

EE Class 40 No. 264 throbs its quiet 16-cylinder beat as it waits for the road north in the down sidings at York (Holgate), 6 June 1973. The train, 6S43, is made up of empty whisky malt hoppers from Belmont Yard at Doncaster for Muir of Ord. [Norman E. Preedy]

INTERPART

BR Class 03 diesel-mechanical shunter No. 03 069 in the sunshine at the southern end of Darlington (Bank Top), acting as station pilot with the help of a superannuated 'conflat' as a temporary shunters' match-truck.
[Brian Morrison]

Class 40 No. 40 069 ambles south through Thirsk with a freight, 12 June 1974. Below, 'Deltic' No. 55 009 *Alycidon* later the same day has a rather more demanding time schedule heading south with an Edinburgh–Kings Cross express. [Brian Morrison]

The changing scene at Darlington, with the passage of years: above, green-liveried 'Deltic' D9017 *The Durham Light Infantry* leaving for the south in June 1965 and (below) No. 55 011 *The Royal Northumberland Fusiliers*, nine years later, with the up 'Tyne-Tees Pullman', 09.12 ex-Newcastle. Changes are apparent in the track and its layout, as well as in the rolling stock.
[Norman E. Preedy/Brian Morrison]

'Deltic' No. 55 005 *The Prince of Wales's Own Regiment of Yorkshire* hurries the down 'Talisman' through the southern approaches to Darlington in June 1974. [Brian Morrison]

9D04
31277

Brush/EE No. 31 277 getting under way from the sidings at Darlington with an unfitted freight for Hull in June 1974.
[Brian Morrison]

Named Class 40 No. 230 *Scythia* on an inter-Regional excursion passing Aycliffe, north of Darlington, in April 1972.
[Norman E. Preedy]

A Class 37 with a six-coach York to Edinburgh semi-fast on the re-aligned curves at Newtonhall in County Durham in 1971. This is one of the examples of the great deal of work that has been done on the East Coast main line to remove obstacles to sustained high-speed running. [Malcolm Dunnett]

A busy scene at Tyne Yard, with Class 37s on freight duties and a Class 45 passing by on the main line with a southbound express. [Malcolm Dunnett]

'Deltic' D9014 *The Duke of Wellington's Regiment* leaving the carriage sidings at Heaton with stock for Newcastle on 14 June 1967. She was the last of the class to remain in this original livery.
[Norman E. Preedy]

A night scene at Newcastle with a Class 47 backing down to take over a fitted freight for across the Border in January 1973. [Malcolm Dunnett]